Crime Stories

Titles in this series:

Crime Stories

Francis Radice

MACMILLAN
PUBLISHERS

© Text Francis Radice 1991
© Illustrations Macmillan Publishers 1991

First published 1991
Reprinted 1993

Published by MACMILLAN PUBLISHERS LTD
London and Basingstoke

Illustrations and cover by Michael Kilraine

Typeset by Macmillan Production Limited

Printed in Singapore

A CIP catalogue record for this book is available from
the British Library

ISBN 0-333-54658-X

Contents

Introduction

This is a collection of four short stories, describing four different kinds of crime: murder, bank robbery, kidnap and theft.

In *Coffins*, four men try to rob a bank, and they have a very good plan to get the money away!

In *Check-out*, six children are left to look after themselves, but there is not enough money to buy food. They know that stealing is wrong, but they have to choose: steal food or go hungry. What are they going to do?

The Dead Body is a story of murder, but where is the body?

Lost is the story of a young boy who is not happy at home. Angry with his parents, he runs away. But the world outside can be a dangerous place.

Coffins

Two men, Fred and Jim, sat in a pub. In front of them, next to their glasses of beer, was a map of Blunderstone, a town in the Midlands in England. Fred lit a cigarette and pointed to something on the map.

'You see, Jim, it's perfect. The bank is next to the grave-yard.'

'But there's nowhere to park the car, Fred,' said Jim.

'Yes, there is. You can park a car right outside the church gate. They let you park there for funerals.'

Jim said, 'I don't think this is a good idea, Fred. Look, there's a police station right opposite the church.'

'That's not a big problem. The funerals are going to help us, Jim. I'll explain to you and the boys down at the church. It's easier to understand my plan down there.'

Fred finished his glass of beer.

'What about the car bringing the other coffin?' said Jim.

'That's another reason why my plan is so perfect, Jim. As I told you, there are two funerals at the church tomor-row: Mrs Mould's funeral and the bank manager's funeral. So no-one in the street will be surprised that there will be two black cars, two coffins, two graves and two groups of friends and families. All the bank staff have got the day off. They won't be at work on Saturday – they are going to be at the bank manager's funeral. The bank is going to be empty. It's brilliant!'

Fred and Jim went out of the pub. They got into their car. The car was a very big black funeral car with a space in the back for carrying a coffin. The two men drove down to Blunderstone and parked the car in a back street near the church. They walked to the church and went into the graveyard. The bank was next to the graveyard and one of its windows looked out over the graves. On the other side of the street, next to the police station, was a café. It was a fine afternoon and the sky was clear.

'Warm, dry weather,' said Fred. 'Just what we want.'

Bernard and Mike were waiting in the church porch. They had pickaxes and spades. They went to a place in the graveyard under the windows of the bank.

'OK,' said Fred. 'Let's start digging.' The men worked, digging the grave, but Fred stood around smoking and watching the street. People were hurrying past, doing their Friday afternoon shopping. Nobody noticed the group of men working near the bank. Soon, there was a good deep hole in the ground.

'Is this hole deep enough, Fred?' asked Jim.

'Go down a bit more, Jim. I can still see the bottom from over here.' They dug for a few minutes more. Soon, the hole was deep enough and Bernard said, 'How about another drink?'

'No,' said Fred. 'No more drinking. We must have clear heads for this work.'

So they went into the Paradise Café for a cup of tea. They sat in one corner and talked about the funerals. Fred asked them.

'Do you all know what to do?'

'What about our coffin?' said Mike. Fred told Mike about the coffin. 'We will bring it in the black car,' he said.

~ ■ ~

At midnight, the big black car drove to the graveyard. This time, there were four men in it. They carried black plastic sacks and in the back of the car was a coffin covered with a brown blanket. It was very dark. Nobody saw them carry the coffin into the graveyard. They put it inside the church. In a few moments they came out and stood in the

shadows, away from the street lights. They were absolutely silent. Each man knew exactly what to do. Fred gave a signal. Bernard and Jim went over to the wall of the bank's backyard. They threw a rope with a hook over the wall and quickly climbed into the yard. Fred and Mike stayed in the churchyard.

Bernard and Jim worked quickly. They stopped the burglar alarm from going off and then they picked the lock of the outside door of the bank and went in. Soon, they found the back of the cash machine. Bernard took out some explosive and set it at the back of the machine. When the door came off, Jim took out the money and put it into one of the plastic sacks.

They went down into the basement and opened some strong-boxes in the same way. Inside the boxes there was silver, gold and jewellery belonging to customers of the bank. There was also a lot of money. Some of the boxes belonged to robbers who had put stolen money in them. Fred knew that money belonging to other robbers was in the boxes. Bernard put all this money and the gold, silver and jewellery into the plastic sacks. They took the sacks upstairs and threw them out of the window and into the grave.

They closed and locked the window carefully, and when they went out of the door they locked that too. Nobody could see anything wrong from the outside of the bank. It was Friday night. The bank staff were out for two days.

'On Monday, they are going to come back and find the money is missing,' said Bernard. 'We have two days to get away.'

In the graveyard, Fred and Mike got down into the grave. Nobody from the street saw them. In a moment they climbed out with the sacks and took them to the church. They opened the coffin and put all the sacks inside and screwed down the lid. Then Bernard and Jim came back from the bank.

'Now we can go home and get some sleep,' said Fred.

~ ∎ ~

At ten o'clock the next morning, the four men came to the funeral of Mrs Mould. They left their car out of sight. The bank manager's funeral was in the afternoon. So the men carrying the coffin with Mrs Mould's body inside were surprised to find another coffin already in the church.

'That's funny!' said one of them, 'The bank manager's coffin is already here.'

'Maybe we've made a mistake about the time,' said another. They put Mrs Mould's coffin down next to the other coffin. They went outside. They wanted to ask the vicar the times of the funerals. Just then, along came Fred and his gang. They were dressed very nicely in black suits and they wore black hats pulled low over their eyes.

'Sorry about the extra coffin,' said Fred. 'It's the bank manager's. We made a mistake about the time. His funeral is this afternoon. We'll take his coffin away.' They went inside the church. The two coffins looked exactly the same.

'This is the one,' said Jim, and they picked it up and carried it out to the car.

'People are going to think this is funny,' said Bernard. 'Usually the coffin goes to the grave in the churchyard. And here we are, putting it into our car.'

'Don't worry, Bernard,' said Fred. Fred knew all the answers.

'Sometimes coffins go to the crematorium.'

'What's a crematorium?' asked Jim.

'Don't you know? It's the place where they cremate people. That means they burn the body. It's called cremation.'

'That's funny. This coffin is very heavy,' said Mike.

'It's all that gold and jewellery inside,' Jim said. 'We didn't waste our time in the bank.'

'Well, this one's not going to the crematorium,' said Mike. 'That's for sure.'

~ ■ ~

The men in the church carried their coffin to the altar for the funeral service.

'This is strange,' said one of them. 'This coffin is very light now.'

'You're forgetting. Mrs Mould was a very small, thin lady,' said another coffin carrier.

~ ■ ~

When Fred's gang arrived at his house, they opened the coffin. They wanted to divide up the money and leave the country. They wanted to go for a long holiday in Brazil. They were hoping to find two million pounds in cash and valuable things. But they did not find two million pounds. Instead, they found the body of Mrs Mould.

They rushed back to the church. They thought the money was buried there. But there was only one grave. It was their grave. It was still empty. They saw the vicar and asked him about Mrs Mould.

'Oh, don't you know?' said the vicar. 'Mrs Mould's coffin went to the crematorium.'

'You mean they're cremating her?' said Fred.

'That's right,' said the vicar. 'They're burning the body of Mrs Mould at this very moment.'

Check-out

My father is a lorry driver and he is often away from home. My mother works at a hotel, so we are sometimes alone in the flat. But I am never lonely because I have five brothers and sisters. My sister, Edith, is the eldest and I am the eldest son. My name is Roger. Edith works in a supermarket and I am looking for a job.

Then there are three more girls, Caron, Sandra and Ruby, who are still at school. The youngest is William. We call him Bird because he always woke us up in the morning when he was a baby. He is still at primary school. Edith and I look after the family because my mother and father are nearly always away from home.

My four sisters do all the housework. Edith does a lot of it when she finishes work. I have to look for a job and so I don't have much time to cook, but I sweep out the rooms once a week. In the afternoon, I go to the primary school and bring Bird home. The three girls walk home at 4.30. We all get our own food and when Edith comes home, she gets the dinner. She says I am the lazy one.

I don't stay at home after dinner. Instead, I go out with my friends. Some of these friends are bad and my mother told me to stay away from them. But they are my friends, so what can I do?

~ ■ ~

Last Monday, a letter came from my Dad. He wrote to my mother, but she was not at home. We thought the letter was important and so we opened it. My Dad wrote,

'I am not coming home, now. I am staying with Sharon in Newcastle.'

Newcastle is a city in the North of England. My Dad often goes there in his lorry.

When she saw the letter, Edith cried. Then we told Caron, Sandra and Ruby, and they cried too. Bird didn't cry because he didn't know our Dad very well anyway.

My father also wrote, 'I am sending you £50 with this letter,' but we could not find the money in the envelope. We think someone took the money.

The supermarket pays Edith at the end of each week. But she had only a little money and we had a lot of bills to pay. Bills are pieces of paper asking for money. We had bills for the rent of the flat, for the gas and electricity. The bills added up to £260.56. Edith had only £7 and we didn't have much to eat.

~ ■ ~

On Tuesday morning, I said to my sisters, 'Don't worry, I am going to think of something.'

They went to school and Edith went to work. I took Bird to school, then went to look for my friends. 'My friends can help me,' I said.

I went down to the river-bank and saw Ted, Jock and Lightning. (His real name is David Smith, but we call him Lightning because he walks so slowly. It takes him half an hour to walk a hundred metres.) They are also looking for work and they sit on the river-bank.

I told these three boys about our trouble at home. The problem was how to get some money quickly. Jock, who is Edith's boyfriend, said,

'You don't need money. You can get food and household things from the shop. At the end of the week, when the supermarket pays Edith, she can pay for the food.' I didn't like this plan, but I said nothing.

We went to the supermarket where Edith worked and I bought some bread, eggs and bacon, cornflakes, milk,

potatoes, cheese, biscuits and sweets. They cost £7.20 and I used Edith's money to pay for them. We went out of the shop past the check-out desk where Edith worked.

Jock said to Edith, 'Let us take these things past you without paying.'

Edith went red in the face. She looked very angry.

She said, 'How can I do that? You're very bad. Get out of here!'

Jock said, 'I am only trying to help you.'

Edith said, 'I don't want your help in that way. Go away and don't come to see me again.'

In the evening, Edith made our dinner. It was a bit difficult to see because there was no light. The electricity company turned the electricity off because we did not pay the bill. It is lucky our cooker is a gas cooker. Edith made our dinner with the potatoes, eggs and bacon. There wasn't enough and we all felt hungry, so we ate the bread and cheese. After that, we ate the sweets.

In the morning, there was not much to eat for breakfast apart from the cornflakes. The postman brought another bill.

'What are we going to have for dinner this evening?' Caron asked.

'Maybe Mum is going to come home, or maybe we can get some money from Dad,' I replied.

~ ■ ~

After breakfast on Wednesday, I sold the TV for £45. The money was just enough to pay the electricity bill, but there was still not enough left over to buy food. That evening, we had only bread and cheese. After supper, I went out to see my friends. They were standing outside a café where they have space games. They had no money.

Jock said, 'Let me talk to Edith.' He came to our flat and talked to her. Edith was angry. But the next day Jock came to our flat with a big bag of food from the supermarket.

I said to Jock, 'I can't pay you for all this food.'

'Don't worry,' said Jock, 'You don't owe me anything. I got it for nothing.'

'Did you steal this food from Edith's supermarket?' I asked.

Jock got angry and said, 'If you don't like this food, I will take it back to the shop.' I thought about dinner for Edith, Caron, Sandra, Ruby and Bird.

I told Jock, 'No, don't take it back,' and he went away.

When Edith came home, she said, 'Jock came into the supermarket and got all this food. He walked past my check-out and he didn't pay for it. I couldn't stop him and I didn't want to get him into trouble, so I said nothing.'

When Edith got her wages at the end of the week, she used the money to pay some of the bills. On Saturday, the only bill left was the one for £115.56 for the rent. The food was enough to last until Wednesday, thanks to Jock. Edith says she is going to pay the supermarket for the food out of her wages. Sandra thinks it is better to keep quiet about it.

We are all worried. There is no news of Mum or Dad. We don't know where Mum is.

On Saturday morning, there was a loud knock on the front door. I went to open it. A policeman stood there.

'I want to speak to your father,' he said.

The Dead Body

One day, Martina found a dead body in the woods. At first she thought it was a man sleeping in the grass. Then she looked more closely and saw the eyes were wide open. Was the man asleep? Martina touched the man's wrist, but nothing happened. She lifted the man's arm and noticed a tattoo of an eagle on the man's hand. The watch on his wrist showed 7.30, long past Martina's suppertime. She let go of the arm and it fell to the ground. Martina thought, 'Perhaps he is pretending to be dead, and he is playing a trick on me.'

Then, suddenly, the man's mouth fell open and she nearly jumped out of her skin. The eyes were wide open, but they did not see her. Now she was sure that the man was dead.

Martina was frightened and she didn't know what to do. She asked herself, 'Shall I call a doctor? Or shall I call the police? Perhaps someone murdered this man and the murderer is hiding nearby. I can call the police, but the murderer might kill me too.' The idea of a doctor made her feel better.

'The doctor can say why the man died,' she thought.

There was no gun or knife on the ground.

'Maybe he was tired after a long walk in the forest and simply wanted to lie in the sun for a rest. Then perhaps he fell asleep and didn't wake up. Sometimes people do that.' Martina's grandfather died like that, she remembered.

The man's clothes were old-fashioned, but clean and neat. His shoes were muddy from walking in the forest. He wore grey trousers, a white shirt, a dark red tie and a green sports jacket. His hair was blond and wavy and he

looked about thirty-five years old. There was a little metal badge on the collar of the jacket. It was like a flag from another country. Martina did not know which country. So the man was a foreigner. Or maybe he came from another country some years before and then stayed in Britain.

Then Martina saw something and her heart jumped. In the inside pocket of the man's clothes, there was a pistol. She got up and hurried back to the streets of the town. 'What can I do?' she said to herself. Then she suddenly thought, 'I was so busy looking at the body that I didn't look carefully at the place where the body lay. I am not even sure I can find the place again.' This worried her, but all the same, she decided to go to the police station.

~ ■ ~

On the way to the centre of the town, Martina saw a policeman. She could tell him about the body.

'Excuse me,' she said. 'There's a body in the woods near here.'

The policeman looked at her in surprise. He said, 'Another kid told me that earlier this evening.' Clearly, the policeman did not believe Martina.

'But there is,' she said. 'It's your job to inspect dead bodies. And I am *not* a kid.'

She was angry with the policeman because he was rude to her. But children often played tricks on this policeman. Once, a small boy told him there was a bag of money behind a wall. He went to look for the bag and of course there was nothing there.

'Perhaps it's someone lying in the grass asleep,' said the policeman.

'But I know the man is dead,' said the girl. 'His arm drops to the ground when you pick it up and his eyes are staring straight ahead without seeing.'

At last the policeman began to believe her.

'I must make sure, anyway,' he thought. Then he said, 'Let's go to the woods and you can show me the exact spot where you found this body.'

They went back to the woods and, at first, Martina could not find the place. She remembered it was in a space among the trees near a big log. When they got there, Martina went round the log and her heart jumped. The body was not there. The policeman got angry.

'You're just like the other children. Why did you bring me here? You're wasting my time.'

He walked away quickly, back towards the town. Just then, Martina looked down and saw something in the grass. It was the man's badge from the collar of his jacket. She picked it up and took it home.

~ ■ ~

The next day, Martina went to the library to look up the flags of the countries of the world. The badge had the colours of the flag of Estonia. She looked in the atlas and saw that Estonia is one of the countries between Russia and the Baltic Sea.

She thought, 'This badge shows I was speaking the truth about the body.'

She decided to go to the police station again and show them the badge. But first, she wanted to look for the body again. 'Maybe I took the policeman to the wrong place,' she thought.

Martina went back to the clearing in the forest. The big log was there and she remembered the place. She walked to the other side of the log and got another shock. The man was there. But this time he was sitting up, leaning against the log. In his right hand was the gun. Martina took a step back. She wanted to run away. She thought the man was pointing the gun at her. Then she remembered the badge and took it out of her pocket.

'Here,' she said. 'You left this in the grass yesterday. I saw you sleeping.' The man didn't answer. Perhaps he was deaf. She spoke louder.

'I've got your badge. You are Estonian, aren't you?'

But the man still did not answer. Then she saw that he was not alive. Someone made him sit up, she thought. Someone put the gun in his hand. Martina ran all the way to the police station and told the man at the desk about the body. She showed him the badge. This policeman was more friendly.

'You are very brave,' he told her, 'and you did the right thing coming here.'

A policewoman drove them to the woods and Martina took them to the clearing. Again, Martina got a shock. There was no body lying in the grass or leaning against the log. But there was a man with blond hair sitting on the log writing in a notebook. He looked up when they came.

'But this is the man I thought was dead,' Martina said. 'Or he looks exactly like the dead man, anyway.'

'Hullo. My name's Menelin,' said the man. 'I'm making a film about Estonians living outside Estonia.'

'We are looking for a dead body,' said the policewoman. 'This young lady saw it here by this log.'

'Oh, that's my model body,' said Menelin. 'I'm using it for my film. We left it in the forest by mistake.'

'You also left this badge,' said Martina, holding it out in her hand. She noticed that Menelin was not wearing a badge. He reached out and tried to grab the badge from her. But the policewoman was quicker.

'I think I'll take that badge, Sir. You can come and collect it at the police station next week.'

The policewoman gave Menelin a receipt for the badge and then drove Martina back to the police station. They sat her down at a table and the policewoman wrote down Martina's story.

Just then, the telephone rang. It was the hospital. They said they had the body of a man. The policewoman took Martina to the hospital. They went to the place where they keep dead bodies and saw something under a white sheet on a table. It was the same body Martina found in the woods. It was not a dummy and there was a tattoo of an eagle on the back of the right hand.

Lost

Tony's father couldn't find his watch. It was time to go to work and he needed his watch.

'Didn't you have it last night?' he said to Tony. 'I saw you in the kitchen and you had the watch then.'

'No, I didn't. That was the kitchen timer.'

'Yes, you did, Tony. You're lying. I saw you with it.'

'Oh, leave the child alone,' said his mother.

'Leave him alone? *You* can talk. You are always angry with him. I'm just looking for my watch.'

'You are too untidy. That's why you're always losing it.'

Tony's father lost his temper.

'Untidy! You say that? Look at the mess this place is in. Clothes on the floor! Jam sticking to the wall! Cornflakes on the carpet! Dirty dishes from last week! Magazines in the kitchen sink! Dirty tissues everywhere! You're a slut, that's what!'

'Get lost!'

'Don't worry. I'm going. And don't cook supper for me this evening. I'm going somewhere for a good meal.' Tony's father went out slamming the door.

'Good! And this evening I'll be out when you come home from the pub!' shouted Tony's mother.

Tony felt miserable. Maybe he did have his father's watch the night before. He couldn't remember. It always started like that. He did something wrong. Then they started fighting.

'It's all because of me,' Tony thought.

'Well, don't just sit around doing nothing!' His mother's voice suddenly shouted at him. 'You're not eating your breakfast. Your shoes aren't on your feet. Your books aren't in your bag and it's time to go to school. You're untidy and half asleep. You didn't go to bed early enough. I'm angry with you, always being late.'

'I'm not always late. This is the first time this week.' (It was Thursday.)

'Don't talk to me like that! And hurry up!'

'I am hurrying, Mum.' He went to his room and then had an idea.

'I'm not coming back this evening. They can shout at each other without me. I'm going to run away.'

~ ■ ~

Tony took the books out of his school bag and packed some clothes in it. In the kitchen, there were some buns, fruit and a can of Coca-Cola. His mother was in the bathroom. Tony put the food in the bag with the clothes and he left the flat quietly.

It was a lovely sunny morning. Everywhere, people hurried to work and they looked happy. Suddenly Tony thought, 'I can't go to school. I haven't got my books.' He thought, 'I know, I can go to London. It's a big city and they can't find you there.' He walked out of town and towards the main road to London.

A small car stopped next to Tony. He thought, 'Now I can get a ride to London.' A woman looked out of the window.

'Where are you going, young man?' He did not like the way she spoke to him.

'I'm going to London. That's where I live.' Tony saw the woman's face. She did not believe him and he was very surprised when she said, 'I'll take you there.'

Halfway to London, the woman stopped the car by the side of the road. She took something out of her bag. Tony felt a needle prick him and then he fell asleep. Later, he woke up in a strange room. He heard a man and a woman talking in the passage. The woman said,

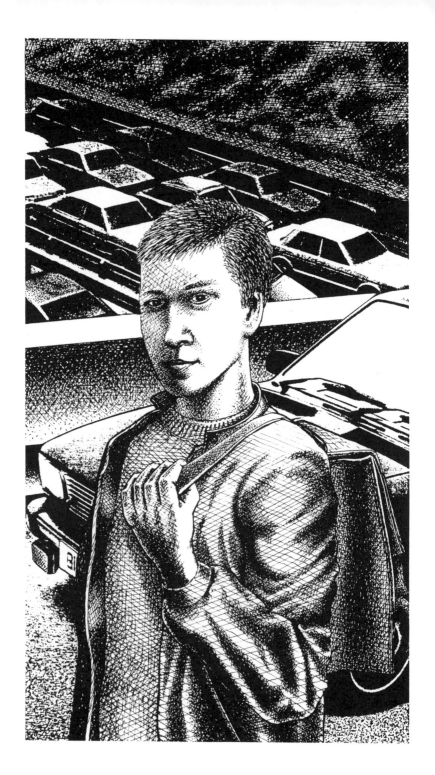

'I'm going to keep him here. His father and mother will pay me.'

'They probably haven't got much money,' said the man. 'He doesn't look as if he has rich parents, so they probably won't pay much for him. Why didn't you get a rich boy?'

'Never mind. I'll cut off his ear and put it in the post. Then they will pay me one thousand pounds.'

Tony jumped up in a fright.

'My parents can't pay one thousand pounds. These people are going to cut off my ear,' he thought.

He went to the window and opened it. He climbed out onto the roof and hid behind a chimney stack. The man and the woman came into the room. Then they ran out to look for Tony in the street. Tony slipped out after they had gone and he ran away quickly.

Soon, he got tired and started walking. He didn't know where he was. He walked around for an hour. London seemed to go on and on for ever. Then he knew he was lost. He came to a hotel and Tony asked how much it cost to stay there. The man said it was twenty pounds a night. Tony had only six pounds.

He got hungry and sat on a wall to eat some food. He did not know what to do. Then he found a strange place. On the door it said 'Centre for Lost People'. Perhaps it was a joke, he thought, but he went in.

The people at the Centre were very nice to Tony.

'We can help you for a few days,' they said. Behind the Centre was a huge, empty office block. The head person in the Centre said,

'You can stay in this building. You must sleep on the floor and keep it clean. It costs thirty pence per night. Each office has many people sleeping in it and a head boy or girl.'

~ ∎ ~

Tony stayed at the Centre for Lost People for several days. Soon, he had no more money left and the Head came to him

and said, 'Can you go back to your home now? Lost people are coming in all the time and there is not enough room. We need your sleeping place.'

Tony said, 'Perhaps I can work here. Then I can stay. I don't want to go back home. My father and mother are always fighting.'

The Head of the Centre said, 'I'm sorry, but we have enough workers already and there is no more room here.'

Tony was very sad. He went upstairs to get his things. He did not know what to do. He didn't want to go home, but there was no other place to go. He came downstairs and went towards the main door.

Suddenly, to his surprise, he saw his father and mother come in. He didn't want them to see him, but he wanted to see and hear them. They went to the reception desk and spoke very quietly. His mother was crying and it was his father who spoke.

'We are looking for a boy called Tony. He is tall and thin and has brown hair and grey eyes. We are very worried. We looked all over the place in Blunderstone. That's where we live. Now we are searching London. The police can't help us. They are too busy.'

Tony's mother cried some more and his father put his arm round her.

'Come on, dear, we'll go back to the hotel. I don't care if it costs us a thousand pounds, but I will find him and bring him home.'

Suddenly, Tony felt happy again. He went to the reception desk. 'You know that man and that woman? They came in here just now,' he said. 'Can you give me the address of their hotel?'

He wrote down the address and went to see the Head of the Centre.

'I think I'm going home now,' he said. 'This is a very good Centre. Thank you for having me.'

Exercises

Coffins

1 What are Fred and Jim going to do?

2 What did the men do in the graveyard?

3 Where did they put the money?

4 What happened to the money?

Check-out

1 Where are the children's parents?

2 How do the boys get food?

3 Does Edith feel happy about this?

4 Who arrives on Saturday morning?

5 What do you think is going to happen?

The Dead Body

1 What did Martina see in the woods?

2 What happened when she went back with a policeman?

3 What did she find the next day?

4 What happened when she took the policewoman there?

5 Where did they find the dead body?

Lost

1 Why does Tony run away?

2 Where does the woman take him? Why?

3 How does Tony escape?

4 Where does he stay?

5 What does he do when he sees his parents?

Glossary

PAGE

4   *basement* (n):   The lowest floor of a building, below the ground
      'They went down into the basement and opened some strong-boxes in the same way.'

1   *brilliant* (adj):   Wonderful
      'It's brilliant!'

11   *check-out desk* (n):   Where people pay in a supermarket
      'We went out of the shop past the check-out desk where Edith worked.'

23   *chimney stack* (n):   The part of a chimney seen above the roof of a building
      'He climbed out onto the roof and hid behind a chimney stack.'

1   *day off* (n):   Holiday
      'All the bank staff have got the day off.'

17   *deaf* (adj):   A person who cannot hear
      'The man didn't answer. Perhaps he was deaf.'

1   *funeral* (n):   A ceremony in church for people who have just died
      'They let you park there for funerals.'

20   *Get lost!*   An impolite way of saying 'Go away'.
      'You're a slut, that's what!' 'Get lost!'

1 **graveyard** (n): The land around a church where dead people are buried
'The bank is next to the graveyard.'

4 **hook** (n): A bent piece of metal used for catching or holding things
'They threw a rope with a hook over the wall and quickly climbed into the yard.'

16 **kid** (n): Child (a slang expression)
'Another kid told me that earlier this evening.'

9 **lightning** (adj): Speed or suddenness
'His real name is David Smith, but we call him Lightning because he walks so slowly.'

17 **log** (n): A thick branch cut or broken off a tree
'She remembered it was in a space among the trees near a big log.'

14 **muddy** (adj): Covered with wet earth
'His shoes were muddy from walking in the forest.'

4 **pick the lock** (v): To open a locked door without a key by using some other instrument
'. . . then they picked the lock of the outside door of the bank and went in.'

2 **pickaxe** (n): A tool for breaking up earth into small pieces
'They had pickaxes and spades.'

2 **porch** (n): The entrance to a church
'Bernard and Mike were waiting in the church porch.'

8 **primary school** (n): In Britain, school for children from 5 to 11 years
'He is still at primary school'

9 **rent** (n): Money paid every week or month for the house you live in

'We had bills for the rent of the flat, for the gas and electricity.'

23 **roof** (n): The covering on top of a building
'He climbed out onto the roof and hid behind a chimney stack.'

16 **rude** (adj): Impolite
'She was angry with the policeman because he was rude to her.'

2 **sack** (n): A very big bag, usually for litter
'They carried black plastic sacks.'

4 **screw** (v): To make the lid of something tight
'They opened the coffin and put all the sacks inside and screwed down the lid.'

4 **in the shadows** (adj): In the dark, away from the light
'They came out and stood in the shadows, away from the street lights.'

20 **slam** (v): To close a door very loudly
'Tony's father went out slamming the door.'

16 **spot** (n): Place
' . . . you can show me the exact spot where you found this body.'

8 **sweep** (v): Brush
'I sweep out the rooms once a week.'

14 **tattoo** (n): A picture done with a needle and ink on a person's body
'She lifted the man's arm and noticed a tattoo of an eagle on the man's hand.'

6 **vicar** (n): A priest in the Church of England
'They wanted to ask the vicar the times of the funerals.'

13 *wages* (n):   Money you get every week for working
    'When Edith got her wages at the end of the week, she used the money to pay some of the bills.'

14 *woods* (n):   A large piece of ground covered with trees
    'One day, Martina found a dead body in the woods.'

Language Grading in the **Macmillan Bookshelf Series**

This reader has been written using a loosely controlled range of language structures. There is no tight control of vocabulary as it is based on the authors' experience of the kind of vocabulary range expected at each particular language level. The authors have also taken care to contextualise any unfamiliar words, which are further explained in the glossary. We hope you will try to deduce meaning from the context, and will use a dictionary where necessary to expand your lexical knowledge.

The language items listed here show those most commonly used at each level in the **Bookshelf** series:

Level One (elementary)
Mainly simple and compound sentences, beginning to use more complex sentences but with limited use of sub clauses

Present Simple	Positive and negative statements
Present Continuous	Interrogative
(present and future reference)	Imperative
Past Continuous	And, or, but, so, because, before, after
'Going to' future	Some/any (-thing)
Past Simple	Basic adjectives
(regular and a few common irregular)	Some common adverbs
Can (ability)	'Simple' comparatives, superlatives
Would like (offer, request)	Gerunds/infinitives, common verbs

Level Two (lower intermediate)
Simple and compound sentences, limited use of complex sentences

Present Perfect	Conditional, can, could (possibility)
Will/won't future	When/while
Present/Past Simple Passive	Question tags, reflexives
Have to, must, should, could	Comparatives, superlatives
Can/may (requests/permission)	(common adjectives/adverbs)
Infinitives (like, want, try, etc.)	Reported speech (present/past)
Gerunds (start, finish, after, like, etc.)	

Level Three (intermediate)
More complex sentences, including embedded clauses

Present Perfect Continuous	Conditionals 1 and 2
Past Perfect	Although, to/in order to, since
Present/Past Continuous Passives	(reason)
Perfect Passives	So/neither
Ought to	Reported statements, requests, etc.
May/might (possibility)	

Level Four (upper intermediate)
At this stage there is minimal control, although authors generally avoid unnecessary complexity

Future Continuous	More complex passives
Past Perfect Continuous	Conditionals 3